Parenting Teen Boys with ADHD

A beginner's guide with practical strategies for behavior management and coping techniques, for Parenting hyperactive teens with ease, love and Logic

By

Stacey R. Sosa

Gain access to more books from me

TABLE OF CONTENTS

Introduction

Parenting is a journey full of pleasure, hardships, and numerous moments that mold our children's lives. When it comes to raising adolescent males, every day is a new experience, and it may be particularly difficult if your son has ADHD. I am excited to begin on this adventure with you, helping you through the unique terrain of parenting adolescent males with ADHD, as someone who has spent years investigating the delicate dance of parenting via the written word.

We'll dig into the interesting world of puberty in this book, where hormones are raging, school hallways are humming, and the need for independence is real. It's a period of self-discovery, progress, and, sure, a few setbacks. When ADHD enters the picture, the road becomes much more complicated.

You may be wondering, "How do I provide the support my teen requires?" How can I assist him in navigating a society that often misunderstands ADHD? Can I actually connect with my kid at this point in his life? The answer is a resounding yes, and I'm here to help you get there.

We'll explore the particular strengths and difficulties of ADHD together as we discover its secrets. We'll travel this terrain together, from laying a firm conceptual foundation to providing you with practical tools. This is more than a book; it's a companion for your parenting journey, providing insights, ideas, and a sympathetic viewpoint.

As a parent, you have a tremendous ability to influence your son's life story. Understanding the complexities of ADHD and refining critical social skills will help him not only succeed but also confidently embrace his personality. This book is your road map, loaded with tales, research-backed guidance, and a dash of levity because, let's face it, laughing is an essential component of any parenting journey.

So, take a cup of your favorite beverage, find a comfortable position, and join me on this voyage. Parenting teen boys with ADHD is a unique experience, and by the conclusion of this book, you'll not only have a better knowledge of your son but also a toolbox of methods to help make this stage of your parenting journey gratifying and enjoyable.

Adolescence is a distinct movement in the symphony of parenting, a crescendo of self-discovery, independence, and progress. When your adolescent child navigates this chaotic melody while also dealing with ADHD, the composition becomes especially complicated. Welcome to the first chapter of our journey into the complex world of parenting teenage boys with ADHD.

A Brief Overview of ADHD in Teen Boys

Statistics and Prevalence:

Let's look at the facts to better comprehend the scenario we're in. ADHD, or Attention Deficit Hyperactivity Disorder, is more than a label for millions of families. According to current figures, around 9% of children aged 2-17 in the United States have ADHD. As we look into this demographic, it's important to remember that these figures reflect not simply numbers, but the faces of countless teens, each with a unique story.

Beyond the statistics, prevalence gives a picture of the common path that many parents take. Our common experiences bind us together, creating a tapestry of understanding and empathy. So, while we dig into the depth of parenting teen boys with ADHD, keep in mind that you are not alone; numerous parents travel this path, experiencing similar obstacles, sharing shared achievements, and learning from one another.

Unique Challenges Teens with ADHD Face

ADHD is not a one-size-fits-all disorder. It appears uniquely in each individual, presenting its mix of challenges and strengths. As we lead our children through the teenage years, we face challenges that are unique for boys with ADHD. These issues go beyond the usual notions of hyperactivity and include difficulty with attention, impulse control, and organization.

The academic landscape becomes a complicated labyrinth, friendships may need more deliberate navigation, and the path to self-discovery might take unexpected detours. Nonetheless, possibilities for growth, resilience, and the development of unique talents exist amid these obstacles. Understanding these problems allows us to adjust our parenting strategy to empower our teenagers, assisting them in overcoming barriers while enjoying their uniqueness.

In the pages that follow, we'll unpack the complexity of ADHD in teenage boys, hoping not just to comprehend but also to appreciate the beauty that difference provides. Let us explore the landscape together, equipped with information, empathy, and a dedication to fostering the potential that each youthful soul has. The path may be difficult, but with understanding as our guide, we can negotiate this chapter of parenting with grace and resilience.

Chapter 1

Understanding ADHD

Parenting is an intricate dance, a symphony of love, direction, and navigating each child's melody. As we begin on this trip, we will meet twists and turns as varied as our children's personalities. The melody may include a few extra staccato notes for parents raising teenage boys with Attention Deficit Hyperactivity Disorder (ADHD), requiring nuanced knowledge and targeted assistance.

In this chapter, we'll get to the heart of the matter: understanding ADHD in the context of parenting adolescent males. Our objective is to provide parents with information that develops empathy, practical techniques, and a meaningful relationship with their boys, from the intricacies of the disorder itself to its tremendous influence on scholastic and social arenas.

In-depth Explanation of ADHD

1. ADHD Types:

a. Inattentive Type (ADHD-I):

ADHD, which is sometimes misinterpreted as a single entity, comprises a range of challenges. The inattentive type, characterized by difficulty sustaining attention, frequent mistakes, forgetfulness, and organizational struggles, paints a vivid picture of a teen who may seem absent-minded or disorganized. Recognizing these characteristics as parents is the first step in tailoring our approach. Creating supportive surroundings, utilizing organizing tools, and comprehending the need for scheduled routines become critical components in leading our ADHD-I boys.

b. Hyperactive-Impulsive Type (ADHD-HI):

On the other end of the spectrum, the hyperactive-impulsive type presents a unique set of challenges. Excessive fidgeting, inability to stay seated, and impulsive behaviors become characteristic markers. Parenting strategies for this type may include directing energy into organized activities, teaching impulse control skills, and fostering environments that allow for their desire for movement.

c. **Combined Type (ADHD-C):** A significant percentage of individuals with ADHD are classified as having both inattentive and hyperactive-impulsive symptoms. This complication necessitates a sophisticated strategy that covers a wide variety of challenges. Understanding the particular combination of features enables parents to adapt therapies, offering tailored help for both attention and hyperactivity issues.

2. Common Symptoms and Behaviors:

a. **Inattention Symptoms:** ADHD's inattentive symptoms go beyond ordinary distractibility. They include difficulty sustaining attention in tasks or play activities, frequent careless mistakes, forgetfulness, and avoidance of tasks requiring prolonged mental effort. Recognizing these signs for parents requires more than just noticing forgetfulness; it also entails comprehending the cognitive barriers that make sustained attention a daily problem.

b. Hyperactivity Symptoms: Hyperactivity, often the stereotype associated with ADHD, manifests as excessive fidgeting, an inability to stay seated, running or climbing in inappropriate situations, and talking excessively. These behaviors are not merely an excess of energy; they are windows into the unique neurobiological processes shaping our teen boys' daily experiences.

c. Impulsivity Symptoms: Impulsivity, a hallmark of ADHD, manifests in various ways. From impatience in waiting for a turn to blurting out answers before questions are completed, the impulsivity symptoms demand a keen understanding. Teaching methods for pausing and thinking before acting becomes critical, providing a buffer against rash judgments that may have long-term implications.

Understanding these symptoms is similar to deciphering a language, allowing parents to engage with their adolescent sons in a more meaningful way. It's not only about regulating behaviors; it's about understanding our boys' unique perspective on the world.

Impact on Teen Development

1. Academic Challenges:

a. Difficulty in Sustaining Focus:

One of the most common challenges that kids with ADHD face is trouble sustaining concentration. Academic assignments that need sustained focus become a battlefield with distractions lurking around every turn. For parents, this entails developing disciplined study routines, dividing tasks into digestible parts, and providing concentration-friendly settings.

b. Organizational Struggles: Forgetfulness and disorganization, characteristic of ADHD, extend their tendrils into academic performance. From misplaced assignments to overlooked deadlines, organizational struggles can hinder effective learning. Parenting strategies include offering organizing tools, cooperating with instructors for specialized help, and instilling a feeling of responsibility in academic commitment management.

c. Impaired Executive Function: ADHD is often associated with difficulties in executive function, which refers to the cognitive processes involved in planning, beginning, and finishing activities. Teens with ADHD may need explicit education in these areas for academic achievement. Breaking down tasks into step-by-step procedures, giving visual aids, and providing continual instruction are all examples of strategies for parenting.

2. Social Struggles:

a. Difficulty in Social Cues:

For teenagers with ADHD, navigating the complex realm of social relationships may be a minefield. Difficulties in reading social signs may lead to misunderstandings and strained relationships. As parents, strengthening social skills becomes a cornerstone of support. Our teen boys are given the tools they need to navigate friendships through social skills training, role-playing common scenarios and open communication about social dynamics.

b. Impulsivity in Social Interactions: The impulsive nature of ADHD can interfere with social interactions. Friendships can be strained by casual remarks or spontaneous actions, so parents must teach strategies to temper impulsivity. Techniques such as "pause and think" become invaluable, allowing teens to interact with others thoughtfully while avoiding unintended social missteps.

c. **Peer Relationships:** Making and maintaining friendships is an essential part of adolescence. This process may necessitate more deliberate guidance for teens with ADHD. Fostering positive social experiences, encouraging participation in shared activities, and providing a supportive environment for social growth are all important parenting strategies in this domain.

Understanding the effect of ADHD on academic and social aspects is about highlighting routes for support and progress, not concentrating on problems. As parents, we become active players in our adolescent boys' growth journeys rather than passive bystanders. In the subsequent chapters, we will look at practical techniques for dealing with these challenges, ensuring that our parenting approach is both knowledgeable and compassionate. Our objective is to equip our adolescent males to traverse adolescence with strength, confidence, and a strong sense of self-worth, not only to comprehend ADHD.

Chapter 2

Parenting Strategies for Teens with ADHD

Parenting is a dynamic adventure, and when ADHD enters the picture, the route takes a distinct and complex turn. In this chapter, we will look at practical solutions for empowering parents who are negotiating the complexity of parenting teenage boys with Attention Deficit Hyperactivity Disorder (ADHD). Our objective is to provide parents with practical methods that encourage development, resilience, and a successful parent-teen connection, from creating a supportive atmosphere to adopting regular routines and positive reinforcement tactics.

Establishing a Supportive Environment

1. Open Communication:

Communication is the foundation of every good relationship, and it is especially important for teenagers with ADHD. Creating a nonjudgmental discussion environment enables for mutual understanding of obstacles, disappointments, and successes. The following are some key communication strategies:

a. **Active Listening:** Practice active listening by providing your complete attention to your adolescent. This builds trust and makes your youngster feel heard and understood.

b. **Empathetic Understanding:** Recognize your teen's particular problems. Empathy goes a long way toward establishing a deep relationship.

Remember that the purpose is to establish an atmosphere in which your adolescent feels comfortable expressing themselves, not only to impart facts.

2. Setting Realistic Expectations:

It is critical to understand the capabilities and problems connected with ADHD to create realistic expectations. Unrealistic expectations may cause parental and teen dissatisfaction and failure. Consider the following approaches:

a. Individualized Goals: Tailor expectations to your teen's unique strengths and challenges. Recognize and appreciate modest triumphs while appreciating the work put in.

b. Collaborative Goal Setting: Involve your teen in the goal-setting process. This fosters a feeling of ownership and self-motivation.

Setting reasonable expectations fosters an atmosphere in which success and development are rewarded.

Implementing Consistent Routines

1. Daily Schedules:

Consistency provides a sense of security for teens with ADHD. Creating and sticking to a daily routine allows you to better manage your time and minimizes worry. Consider the following approaches:

a. Visual Schedules: Create visual schedules or use apps to help your teen visualize daily routines. This improves predictability and reduces surprises.

b. Morning and Evening Routines: Create regular morning and evening routines. Steps that are clearly defined assist your adolescent in transitioning seamlessly between tasks.

A defined daily schedule not only helps your adolescent manage his or her time but also develops stability.

2. Homework and Study Routines:

Academic assignments may be difficult for teenagers with ADHD. Consistent homework and study habits are essential for success. Here are several techniques that work:

a. **Designated Study Spaces:** Create a distraction-free, peaceful study place. This allows your adolescent to concentrate on the work at hand.

b. **Chunking Tasks:** Break down assignments into smaller, manageable tasks. This method makes the burden less daunting.

c. **Scheduled Breaks:** Incorporate short breaks during study sessions. This helps to minimize burnout and retain concentration.
Consistent and planned study habits enable your kid to better manage academic duties.

Positive Reinforcement Techniques

1. Reward Systems:

Positive reinforcement is a potent tool for behavior modification. The use of incentive systems fosters desirable behaviors and pushes your adolescent to take on new tasks. Consider the following approaches:

a Clear and Achievable Goals: Set clear and achievable goals for your teen. Celebrate accomplishments, large or small, with meaningful awards.

b. Consistent Reinforcement: Provide positive reinforcement regularly. Predictable incentives reinforce the link between effort and favorable results.
A well-structured incentive system fosters a feeling of success and motivation by creating a positive feedback loop.

2. Fostering Independence and Responsibility:

Fostering independence is an important component of parenting ADHD kids. Encouragement of responsibility boosts confidence and prepares your adolescent for the responsibilities of maturity. Here are some techniques for encouraging independence:

a. Gradual Increase in Responsibilities: Gradually increase your teen's responsibilities at home. Chores, self-care responsibilities, and maintaining personal calendars are examples of this.

b. Problem-Solving Discussions: Participate in problem-solving talks with your adolescent. Encourage them to consider problems and possible solutions critically.

Giving your adolescent a feeling of freedom instills confidence in their talents and boosts their self-esteem.

Chapter 3

Building Essential Social Skills

Navigating the complicated world of social relationships is a universal struggle for teens, and the difficulties increase when Attention Deficit Hyperactivity Disorder (ADHD) is present.

This chapter goes into the critical area of developing crucial social skills for parents of ADHD teenage boys. Our research intends to provide parents with practical solutions for nourishing their boys' social development throughout this critical stage of adolescence, ranging from communication and conflict resolution to emotional control and team-building activities.

Social Skills Training

1. Communication Skills:

Successful social connections are built on effective communication. Due to impulsivity and difficulty picking up social signs, teenagers with ADHD may have communication difficulties. Here are some techniques for improving communication skills:

a. Active Listening: Teach your adolescent how to listen actively. To exhibit participation, encourage them to concentrate on the speaker, ask clarifying questions, and give feedback.

b. Non-Verbal Cues: Emphasize the importance of non-verbal cues, such as eye contact and body language. These small cues aid in efficient communication.

c. Social Scripts: Provide your teen with social scripts for common scenarios. This makes it easier for them to navigate discussions.

Teens with ADHD may strengthen their connections with their classmates and develop meaningful interactions by refining their communication skills.

2. Conflict Resolution Strategies:

Conflicts are an unavoidable element of social relationships, and conflict resolution is an important skill to acquire. Impulsivity may exacerbate conflict situations in teenagers with ADHD. Provide your adolescent with dispute resolution methods such as:

a. Pause and Reflect: Teach your teen to pause and reflect before responding impulsively to conflicts. This stops the situation from escalating.

b. Use "I" Statements: Encourage the use of "I" statements to express feelings without placing blame. This encourages free conversation and comprehension.

c. Negotiation Skills: Advice about negotiating and compromising. Teens may learn to establish common ground and collaborate to achieve mutually beneficial outcomes.

Conflict resolution tactics not only help to diffuse uncomfortable situations, but they also help to build strong interpersonal skills.

Emotional Regulation Techniques

1. Recognizing and Managing Emotions:

Emotional control is a fundamental ability that has an impact on social relationships. Teens with ADHD may struggle to recognize and manage their emotions. Here are some ways to help with emotional regulation:

a. Emotion Identification: Assist your adolescent in recognizing and labeling their emotions. This level of self-awareness is required for efficient emotional control.

b. Mindfulness Practices: Introduce mindfulness techniques to help your teen stay present and manage overwhelming emotions.

Encourage the use of emotional diaries for tracking and reflecting on emotions. This improves one's emotional intelligence.

Teens may approach social situations with better control and resilience if they practice emotional management skills.

2. Coping Mechanisms for Stress and Frustration:

Stress and frustration are common triggers for difficulties in social interactions. It is critical to provide teenagers with adequate coping techniques. Consider the following approaches:

a. Deep Breathing Exercises: Teach deep breathing exercises to help your teen manage stress and anxiety in real time.

b. Physical Activities: Encourage participation in physical activities to relieve stress and frustration.

c. Positive Self-Talk: Develop the practice of using positive self-talk to combat negative ideas and cultivate a resilient attitude.

Coping techniques enable adolescents to negotiate the ups and downs of social circumstances with poise and adaptation.

Team Building Activities

1. Group Projects and Collaborations:

Participating in group projects promotes cooperation and teamwork. This provides a chance for kids with ADHD to practice and improve their social skills in an organized setting. Consider the following approaches:

a. Role Assignments: To create structure and avoid overload, clearly identify responsibilities within the group.

Encourage frequent check-ins to verify that everyone is on the same page. This encourages clear communication and problem-solving.

Recognize and celebrate the group's accomplishments to reinforce the importance of teamwork.

Group projects not only help with academic improvement, but they also act as social labs for the development of important skills.

2. Involvement in Extracurricular Activities:

Extracurricular activities provide a rich tapestry of social chances. From sports to clubs, participating in organized extracurricular activities offers a supportive environment for social skill development. Here's how to get the most out of it:

a. **Identify Interests:** Encourage your adolescent to participate in extracurricular activities that are related to their interests. This increases motivation and involvement.

b. **Social Coaching:** Provide advice on social dynamics within the selected activity. This might include tactics for establishing new acquaintances and successfully cooperating.

Consistent participation is essential. Regular participation in extracurricular activities gives continuing social practice and exposure.

Extracurricular activities not only enhance your teen's life but also provide a dynamic field for social development.

Chapter 4

Collaborating with Schools and Professionals

Parenting teens with Attention Deficit Hyperactivity Disorder (ADHD) is a team effort that goes outside the household. Schools and professionals play critical roles in assisting teenagers with ADHD with their academic, emotional, and social development.

This chapter examines ways for successful cooperation, stressing open communication, collaborating with instructors, and obtaining professional assistance when necessary. Parents may construct a thorough support system for their children by creating strong links with schools and experts.

Communicating with Teachers

1. Creating a Partnership with Educators:

Building a collaborative partnership with teachers is fundamental to your teen's academic success. Opening avenues of communication provide a way for mutual understanding and support. Here are some excellent methods for encouraging collaboration:

a. Initiate Regular Communication: Schedule regular check-ins with teachers to discuss your teen's progress, challenges, and successes. This continuing conversation keeps you up to date on intellectual concerns.

b. Share Insights About ADHD: Educate instructors on ADHD and provide them with information about your teen's specific strengths and struggles. This collaborative approach creates empathy and a shared commitment to the achievement of your kid.

c. Work Together on Accommodations: Work together to discover and implement academic adjustments that are appropriate for your teen's learning style. This might include more time for assignments, preferred seating, or access to assistive technology.

The goal is to approach instructors as partners in creating an optimum learning environment for your adolescent.

2. Advocating for Your Teen's Needs:

Advocacy is an important part of working with schools. You are your teen's most powerful advocate as a parent. Here are some tips for successfully advocating for your teen's needs:

a. Develop an Individualized Education Program (IEP) or 504 Plan: Work with the school's special education staff to create an IEP or 504 plan for your adolescent that specifies specific adjustments and support services. This legal document guarantees that your teen's special needs are met in the classroom.

b. Request Regular Updates: Keep up to date on your teen's academic achievement. Regular teacher reports, along with a collaborative approach, enable prompt response if problems occur.

c. Participate in Parent-Teacher Conferences: Participate actively in parent-teacher conferences to discuss your adolescent's academic and social progress. This gives a chance to address problems, exchange ideas, and emphasize the necessity of working together.

Advocacy is proactive participation with the school community to ensure that your teen's educational experience is suited to their specific need.

Seeking Professional Assistance

1. Counseling and Therapy Alternatives:

A teen's emotional and behavioral well-being, in addition to academic help, is critical to his or her total growth. Seeking professional help, such as counseling or therapy, may be an important part of managing your teen's ADHD. Consider the following approaches:

a. Identify Qualified Professionals: Seek licensed counselors or therapists with experience in working with teens with ADHD. They may provide useful insights and solutions for dealing with the emotional components of the disease.

b. Collaborate with School Counselors: Make use of the school's counseling services. School counselors may provide extra assistance and coordinate with other specialists to achieve a comprehensive strategy.

c. Promote Open Communication: Encourage open communication among counseling providers, schools, and families. Regular updates and goal-setting collaboration improve the efficacy of therapeutic approaches.

Professional guidance increases your teen's emotional resilience, allowing them to negotiate the obstacles of adolescence with increased self-awareness.

2. Medication Management Discussions:

Medication may be prescribed as part of the treatment strategy for certain teenagers with ADHD. It is critical to engage in open and informed talks with healthcare experts. Consider the following approaches:

a. **Consult a Specialist:** Seek advice from healthcare specialists who specialize in the treatment of ADHD. Pediatricians, child psychiatrists, and ADHD experts may be included.

b. **Educate Yourself on Medication Alternatives:** Learn about the numerous pharmaceutical alternatives available for ADHD therapy. Understanding the possible advantages and disadvantages enables you to make educated choices in partnership with healthcare providers.

c. **Maintain Continuous Communication:** Maintain an open channel of contact with the prescribing physician. Regular check-ins aid in monitoring the efficacy of the drug and addressing any issues as soon as possible.
Medication management talks should be done collaboratively, taking into account both healthcare experts' and your teen's experiences.

Chapter 5

Addressing Co-occurring Challenges

Parenting a teen with Attention Deficit Hyperactivity Disorder (ADHD) entails negotiating a complex environment of difficulties. Aside from the fundamental symptoms of ADHD, many teenagers also struggle with co-occurring conditions, which can have a substantial influence on their general well-being.

In this chapter, we look at typical co-occurring issues like anxiety, depression, and learning difficulties, as well as holistic treatment techniques. Parents can establish a supportive environment that encourages their teen's holistic development by knowing and addressing these co-occurring difficulties.

Common Co-occurring Conditions

1. Depression and Anxiety:

Teens with ADHD are at a higher risk of developing anxiety and sadness. ADHD symptoms, academic pressures, and social dynamics can all play a role in these mental health issues. Here are some methods for recognizing and dealing with anxiety and depression:

a. Observing Behavioral Changes: Be attentive to changes in your teen's behavior, mood, or social interactions. Withdrawal, irritability, and changes in sleeping patterns can all be symptoms of anxiety or depression.

Create a secure space for your teen to express their emotions through open communication. Encourage them to talk openly about their experiences, anxieties, and stressors.

b. Professional Intervention: Seek the advice of mental health specialists who specialize in treating adolescents, such as therapists or counselors. Professional assistance can offer coping skills as well as therapeutic measures.

Anxiety and depression require a multifaceted strategy that includes both emotional support and professional help.

2. Learning Disabilities:

Learning disabilities often co-occur with ADHD, presenting additional challenges in the academic realm. Understanding and addressing these learning difficulties is critical for ensuring that your kid receives appropriate assistance. Consider the following approaches:

a. Comprehensive Educational Assessment: Collaborate with educators to carry out a thorough educational assessment. This aids in the identification of specific learning impairments and the development of customized therapies.

b. Individualized Learning Strategies: Collaborate with the school to develop tailored learning plans that take into account your teen's distinct learning style. This could involve extra assistance in specific subjects, customized assignments, or assistive technology.

c. Accommodation Advocacy: During standardized testing, advocate for adjustments that address learning challenges. This ensures that your teen has a fair chance to exhibit their expertise.

Parents can establish a supportive academic atmosphere that increases their teen's learning experience by treating learning difficulties with ADHD.

Holistic Approaches to Treatment

1. Nutrition and Lifestyle Adjustments:

The importance of nutrition and lifestyle in managing ADHD and co-occurring disorders is becoming more widely recognized. A comprehensive strategy that incorporates nutritional considerations and lifestyle changes can help with general well-being. Here are some techniques for integrating nutrition and lifestyle changes:

a. **Balanced Diet:** Make sure your teen eats a well-balanced and nutritious diet. Omega-3 fatty acids, found in fish and flaxseeds, have been demonstrated to offer potential benefits for people with ADHD.

Encourage frequent physical activity because it has been linked to increased attention and mood. Sports, yoga, and even everyday walks can all have a favorable impact.

b. Adequate Sleep: Make good sleep habits a priority. Sleep deprivation can aggravate ADHD symptoms and lead to mood issues. Maintain a consistent sleep schedule to promote general well-being.

Nutrition and lifestyle changes help to build a holistic basis for controlling ADHD and its co-occurring issues.

2. Mindfulness and Relaxation Techniques:

Mindfulness techniques are becoming more well-acknowledged for their potential to help people with ADHD and co-occurring diseases. These methods encourage self-awareness, emotional regulation, and stress reduction.

Consider the following approaches:

a. **Mindful Breathing:** Teach your teen how to breathe mindfully to handle stress and anxiety. Simple techniques like deep belly breathing can be done anywhere.

b. **Guided Meditation:** Introduce teen-friendly guided meditation or mindfulness apps. These services frequently offer structured workshops to assist users in cultivating a mindful mindset.

c. **Yoga and Relaxation:** Learn about yoga and relaxation techniques. These practices combine physical activity and mindfulness to provide a comprehensive approach to well-being.

By adding mindfulness and relaxation practices into daily activities, parents can provide their teenagers with vital tools for stress management and mental health promotion.

Chapter 6

Success Stories and Case Studies

Parenting a teen with ADHD provides unique challenges, but it is also distinguished by incredible successes and success stories.

In this chapter, we look at real-life instances of parental practices that have resulted in beneficial outcomes and highlight the remarkable accomplishments of ADHD youth. We hope to inspire and motivate parents by studying these success stories and case studies, demonstrating that with the correct support and methods, kids with ADHD can traverse adolescence with resilience and realize their full potential.

Real-life Examples of Parenting Strategies

1. Individualized Support Plans: The Johnson Family Case Study

The Johnsons encountered the challenges of raising a teenage kid with ADHD, Alex. Recognizing the need for individualized support, they collaborated with Alex's school to create a comprehensive Individualized Education Program (IEP). This strategy contained specific amenities such as extra time for assignments, privileged seating, and exam access to a quiet space.

Parenting Strategies:

Advocacy: The Johnsons actively advocated for their son, ensuring that his special needs were recognized and met in the school setting.

Regular Communication: The family communicated with teachers regularly to monitor progress and make any revisions to the assistance plan.

Celebrating Progress: By acknowledging and celebrating Alex's achievements, no matter how small, the Johnsons fostered a positive and supportive environment at home.

Outcome:

Alex's academic performance increased substantially, and he gained confidence and self-esteem. His achievement was built on a customized assistance plan.

2. Creating Structured Routines: The Patel Case Study:

The Patel family dealt with the difficulties of raising their adolescent son, Aryan, who has ADHD. Recognizing the need for structure, they established regular daily routines at home. This included set study times, regular food schedules, and well-organized storage areas for goods.

Parenting Strategies:

Creating Predictable Routines: The Patels devised visual calendars and checklists to assist Aryan in predictably navigating his daily activities.

Encourage Independence: By gradually delegating responsibility, Aryan gained independence and ownership over his routine.

Flexibility with Adaptations: While maintaining structure, the family remained flexible, allowing for adaptations based on Aryan's evolving needs.

Outcome:

Aryan's time management and task management abilities improved, leading to a more structured and focused approach to both academic and personal duties.

Notable Achievements of ADHD Teens

1. Academic Success: Jason's Journey
Case Study:

Jason, a teen with ADHD, struggled academically, which affected his self-esteem. His parents worked with educators to create targeted interventions such as customized tutoring and reduced homework.

Parenting Strategies:

Recognizing and fostering Jason's Strengths: Jason's parents focused on identifying and fostering his strengths, such as creativity and problem-solving abilities.

Tutoring Support: Engaging the services of a tutor with expertise in ADHD helped Jason tackle specific academic hurdles.
Jason's confidence in his academic talents improved as a result of regular support and reinforcement of his accomplishments.

Jason not only overcame academic difficulties, but he also acquired a love for computer programming. His success in coding competitions became a source of pride and motivation for him.

2. Social and Emotional Development: Emma's Empowerment

Emma, an ADHD adolescent, had difficulty with social connections and emotional stability. Her parents used a diverse approach that included therapy, social skills training, and extracurricular activities.

Parenting Strategies:

Emma received therapeutic support in order to develop coping mechanisms for anxiety and emotional regulation.

Emma received real tools for handling social encounters after participating in rigorous social skills training classes.

Extracurricular Activities: Emma's participation in a theatrical group not only matched her interests but also served as a platform for creating social relationships.

Outcome:

Emma's heightened emotional intelligence and social abilities resulted in meaningful friendships and self-confidence.

Chapter 7

Community Support and Resources

Parenting a teen with Attention Deficit Hyperactivity Disorder (ADHD) is a rewarding adventure that is significantly aided by a supportive community and helpful resources.

In this chapter, we will look at the importance of community support and the abundance of resources available to parents who are negotiating the specific challenges of raising ADHD-affected teen boys. These outlets play an important role in empowering parents and developing a sense of solidarity, from connecting with other parents through support groups to obtaining educational materials such as books and online courses.

Connecting with Other Parents

1. Forums and support groups:

Parenting, especially when dealing with the intricacies of ADHD, can feel isolating at times. The power of community, on the other hand, resides in interacting with people who have had comparable experiences. Parents can share their struggles, achievements, and ideas in support groups and online forums.

Benefits of Support Groups:

Mutual Understanding: Connecting with other parents facing similar issues provides a sense of affirmation and understanding.

Exchange of Practical Advice: Support groups can be used to share practical solutions that have worked for other families.

Emotional Support: Knowing that you are not alone in your experiences can be comforting at difficult times.

Online Forums:

ADDitude Forums: Platforms like ADDitude offer online forums where parents can engage in discussions, seek advice, and share their stories.

Understood Community: The Understood community connects parents, shares resources, and gives support.

2. Sharing Experiences and Advice:

The power of shared experiences cannot be overstated. Parents who have faced comparable difficulties can provide helpful insights and guidance based on their experiences.

Local Parenting Groups:

Local Meetups: Look into local parenting groups that specialize in ADHD. Meetups allow you to interact in person with other parents in your town.

School-based Parent Organizations: Many schools have parent organizations where you can meet other parents, share experiences, and work together on projects.

Benefits of Sharing Experiences:

Practical Advice: Learning from the experiences of others might provide practical advice for dealing with certain situations.

Creating a Support Network: Making relationships with other parents helps to build a support network that goes beyond online interactions.

Sharing experiences can help break down the stigma associated with ADHD and encourage understanding.

Accessing Educational Materials

1. **Books, podcasts, and documentaries:** Educational materials are critical in providing

parents with the knowledge and methods they need to overcome the obstacles of parenting ADHD teens. Books, podcasts, and documentaries all provide unique viewpoints and ideas.

Recommended Books:

"The Explosive Child" by Ross W. Greene: This book takes a caring and collaborative approach to parenting children who exhibit challenging behavior.

"Driven to Distraction" by Edward M. Hallowell and John J. Ratey: The authors provide practical guidance as well as personal tales to assist parents in understanding and supporting their ADHD-affected teens.

Documentaries and podcasts:

ADDitude's "ADHD Experts Podcast" provides professionals discussing various areas of ADHD, providing helpful insights for parents.

Documentary "Failing at Normal": This documentary examines the lives of people with

ADHD, shedding light on their particular talents and challenges.

2. Online Courses and Workshops:

In the digital era, online courses and workshops give parents accessible and flexible ways to enhance their understanding of ADHD and gain practical skills.

Reputable Online Platforms:

CHADD (Children and Adults with Attention-Deficit/Hyperactivity Disorder): CHADD provides online courses, webinars, and resources for parents who want to learn more about ADHD.

Udemy and Coursera: These platforms frequently feature courses on ADHD, parenting techniques, and other related issues.

Benefits of Online Courses:

Flexibility: Online courses enable parents to learn at their own pace, allowing them to integrate education into their hectic schedules.

Expert Guidance: Many online courses are developed by experts in the field, providing reliable and evidence-based information.

Interactive Learning: Some platforms, such as forums or Q&A sessions, allow parents to communicate with teachers and other participants.

Chapter 8

The Road Ahead: Preparing for Adulthood

As parents of adolescent boys with Attention Deficit Hyperactivity Disorder (ADHD), the path includes not just navigating adolescent issues but also preparing for the transition to adulthood.

This chapter looks ahead, concentrating on vital issues including transitioning to independence, college and career readiness, and the development of critical life skills. By proactively addressing these issues, parents can equip their ADHD-affected children to face adulthood with confidence and resilience.

Transitioning to Independence

1. College and Career Readiness:

The transition to adulthood often involves decisions about higher education and career paths. This shift may necessitate more planning and assistance for youth with ADHD in order to facilitate a successful move into independence.

Navigating the College Landscape:

Choosing the Right Environment: Work with your teen to identify college environments that provide ADHD support programs. Tutoring programs, counseling services, and easily available resources may be included.

Understanding Accommodations: Learn about the accommodations available in college settings for you and your teen. This could include more testing time, note-taking assistance, or dedicated study areas.

Building Self-Advocacy Skills: Assist your teen in developing self-advocacy skills. This entails

defining their needs, successfully engaging with teachers, and utilizing available resources.
Preparing for Careers:

Exploring Interests and Strengths: Work with your teen to identify and develop their interests and strengths. This investigation can help them make professional choices that are in line with their interests.

Internships & Work Experience: Encourage students to participate in internships or part-time jobs linked to their future careers. This gives you hands-on experience and helps you establish your professional network.

Resume Building: Help your kid create a thorough CV that showcases their abilities, accomplishments, and relevant experiences.

2. Life Skills Development:

Adult independence necessitates the development of vital life skills in addition to academic and job success. Teens with ADHD may benefit from individualized instruction in developing these abilities.

Financial Literacy:

Budgeting: Teach your teen budgeting skills while emphasizing the need for fiscal responsibility. Introduce terms like income, expenses, and savings.

Online banking and transactions: Make sure your kid understands fundamental financial procedures and Internet transactions. Understanding statements, utilizing ATMs, and managing accounts digitally are all part of this.

Credit Management: Provide information on how to use credit responsibly. Discuss the consequences of credit ratings, interest rates, and the significance of timely payments.

Time Management:

Use of Planners and Apps: Introduce time management tools such as planners or mobile apps. Encourage the use of calendars for tasks, deadlines, and appointment scheduling.

Setting Priorities: Help your teen establish priorities. Assist them in distinguishing between urgent and critical jobs and developing time management skills.

Breaking Down Tasks: Teach the skill of breaking down larger tasks into smaller, manageable steps. This helps to avoid overburden and assures development.

Nutrition and cooking:

Basic Cooking Skills: Teach your teen the fundamentals of cooking. Meal planning, food shopping, and making easy and nutritious meals are all part of this.

Understanding Nutrition: Discuss nutrition basics, emphasizing the significance of a well-balanced diet. Give practical advice on how to make healthy dietary choices.

Meal Preparation Techniques: Share meal preparation ideas, such as batch cooking or using meal kits.

Communication and Interpersonal Skills:

Discussion and modeling of effective conflict resolution tactics. Instill the value of active listening, gently expressing oneself, and finding mutually beneficial solutions.

Networking principles and tactics: Introduce networking principles and tactics. Assist your kid in understanding the importance of professional contacts and how to create and maintain a network.

Social Etiquette: Provide advice on social etiquette in a variety of circumstances, from professional settings to social events.

Conclusion

Parenting teenagers is a transforming experience with highs and lows as well as distinct challenges. When negotiating this path with adolescent boys who have Attention Deficit Hyperactivity Disorder (ADHD), the journey becomes even more complicated.

We reflect on the comprehensive tactics, ideas, and experiences offered throughout this guide in this last chapter. We'll go over critical tactics again, give parents support, and underline the necessity of celebrating achievement while enjoying the ongoing journey of parenting ADHD kids.

Recap of Key Strategies:

1. Understanding ADHD:

In-depth Knowledge: Effective parenting practices are built on a solid grasp of ADHD, including its types, common symptoms, and developmental consequences.

Individualized Approach: Recognizing your teen's ADHD profile's particular strengths and weaknesses enables the development of tailored assistance plans.

2. Parenting Strategies for ADHD Teens:

Creating a Supportive Environment: Open communication, fair expectations, and a supportive home atmosphere all contribute to your teen's happiness.
Daily routines, homework routines, and consistent frameworks help to give stability and encourage successful time management.

Positive Reinforcement Techniques: Using reward systems and fostering independence promotes motivation and a positive attitude.

3. Building Essential Social Skills:

Social Skills Training: Learning effective communication and conflict resolution skills gives kids the tools they need to navigate social situations.

Emotional Regulation Techniques: Recognizing and controlling emotions, as well as stress-coping methods, all contribute to emotional well-being.

Team Building Activities: Participation in group projects and extracurricular activities promotes social development and a sense of belonging.

4. Collaborating with Schools and Professionals:

Communicating with Teachers: Collaborating with educators, advocating for your teen's needs, and participating in regular updates all contribute to academic success.

Seeking Professional Help: Counseling, therapy choices, and discussions about medication control are all important parts of comprehensive ADHD care.

5. Addressing Co-Occurring Issues:

Common Co-occurring Conditions: Recognizing and treating disorders including anxiety, depression, and learning difficulties is critical for overall health.

Holistic Treatment Approaches: Nutrition, lifestyle changes, mindfulness, and relaxation techniques all contribute to effective ADHD control.

6. Success Stories and Case Studies:

Real-life Examples of Parenting Strategies: Success stories include individualized assistance plans, organized routines, and rewarding achievement.

Notable Achievements of ADHD Teens: Academic performance, social and emotional development, and personal accomplishments demonstrate the potential for positive results.

7. Community Resources and Support:

Making Friends with Other Parents: Support groups, internet forums, and exchanging experiences foster a sense of community and comprehension.

Accessing Educational Materials: Books, podcasts, documentaries, online courses, and workshops are all excellent sources of continuing education.

8. The Road Ahead: Adulthood Preparation:

Transitioning to Self-Sufficiency: College and job readiness, as well as the development of life skills, establish the groundwork for a smooth transition to adulthood.

Encouragement for Parents

1. Celebrating Progress:

Parenting teens with ADHD is a journey marked by incremental progress and achievements. Parents must recognize these modest successes. Recognizing and praising your teen's efforts and growth promotes a healthy and supportive environment.

Recognizing Efforts: Acknowledge the effort your teen puts into managing their ADHD, whether it's completing a challenging assignment or employing a new coping mechanism.

Highlighting Strengths: Concentrate on your teen's abilities and capabilities. Celebrate accomplishments that demonstrate their strengths and potential.

Setting Realistic Expectations: Recognize that development may come in little steps, and setting realistic expectations helps you and your teen avoid needless stress.

2. Embracing the Journey of Parenting ADHD Teens:

Parenting is an evolving process, and it is critical to embrace the journey with compassion, resilience, and a growth mentality. Recognize that difficulties are opportunities for learning and that your dedication to your teen's well-being has a huge impact.

Adapting Strategies: Be open to adapting parenting strategies based on your teen's changing needs. A dynamic and supportive parenting strategy benefits from adaptability and flexibility.

Asking for Help: Keep in mind that asking for help is a sign of strength, not weakness. Increase your support network by connecting with other parents, professionals, and community resources.
Prioritize self-care in order to maintain your well-being. Self-care allows you to be a more productive and patient parent.

Parenting adolescent boys with ADHD is a difficult journey that demands commitment, comprehension, and continual education. While each family's experience is unique, the tactics, thoughts, and anecdotes provided in this guide emphasize the significance of a comprehensive and personalized approach.

As you navigate the challenges and celebrate the successes, remember that you are not alone. Parenting ADHD kids is a shared experience, and by learning from one another, modifying tactics, and adopting a growth mindset, you can build a supportive atmosphere for both yourself and your teen.

The road ahead may be bumpy, but by understanding ADHD, implementing effective methods, and cultivating a positive and resilient mentality, you empower your teen to thrive throughout adolescence and beyond. Embrace the journey, appreciate the accomplishments, and continue to be a guiding force in your teen's life, helping them on their journey to maturity.

www.ingramcontent.com/pod-product-compliance
Lightning Source LLC
Chambersburg PA
CBHW050746260726
48661CB00001B/443